HISTORY OF PETS

THE HISTORY OF PET FISH

by Alicia Z. Klepeis

pogo

Ideas for Parents and Teachers

Pogo Books let children practice reading informational text while introducing them to nonfiction features such as headings, labels, sidebars, maps, and diagrams, as well as a table of contents, glossary, and index.

Carefully leveled text with a strong photo match offers early fluent readers the support they need to succeed.

Before Reading

- "Walk" through the book and point out the various nonfiction features. Ask the student what purpose each feature serves.
- Look at the glossary together. Read and discuss the words.

Read the Book

- Have the child read the book independently.
- Invite him or her to list questions that arise from reading.

After Reading

- Discuss the child's questions. Talk about how he or she might find answers to those questions.
- Prompt the child to think more. Ask: Do you have a pet fish or know someone who does? Do you think fish make good pets? Why or why not?

Pogo Books are published by Jump!
5357 Penn Avenue South
Minneapolis, MN 55419
www.jumplibrary.com

Library of Congress Cataloging-in-Publication Data

Names: Klepeis, Alicia, 1971- author.
Title: The history of pet fish / by Alicia Z. Klepeis.
Description: Minneapolis, MN: Jump!, Inc., [2024]
Series: History of pets | Includes index.
Audience: Ages 7-10
Identifiers: LCCN 2023002462 (print)
LCCN 2023002463 (ebook)
ISBN 9798885246132 (hardcover)
ISBN 9798885246149 (paperback)
ISBN 9798885246156 (ebook)
Subjects: LCSH: Ornamental fishes—History—Juvenile literature.
Classification: LCC SF457.25 .K54 2024 (print)
LCC SF457.25 (ebook)
DDC 639.3—dc23/eng/20230215
LC record available at https://lccn.loc.gov/2023002462
LC ebook record available at https://lccn.loc.gov/2023002463

Editor: Eliza Leahy
Designer: Molly Ballanger

Photo Credits: Michael Gray/Dreamstime, cover (plants), cover (goldfish); TeoLazarev/iStock, cover (castle); Shutterstock, cover (tropical fish); Image Source Collection/Shutterstock, 1; koifish/Shutterstock, 3; Michael Grubka/Alamy, 4; Nomad_Soul/Shutterstock, 5; Dany Kurniawan/Shutterstock, 6; Tatsuo Nakamura/Shutterstock, 7; Peter Unger/Getty, 8-9 (top); chechele/iStock, 8-9 (bottom); Heritage Images/Getty, 10-11; Mirko_Rosenau/iStock, 12-13, 22tr, 22ml, 22br; LuFeeTheBear/Shutterstock, 14 (top); The Image Party/Shutterstock, 14 (bottom); Last ever/iStock, 15; Panupon Eurawong/Shutterstock, 16-17; Sergiy Akhundov/Shutterstock, 18-19; simonlong/Getty, 20-21; panpilai paipa/Shutterstock, 22tl; Napat/Shutterstock, 22mr, 22bl; Andrei Dubadzel/Shutterstock, 23 (left); Ja Crispy/Shutterstock, 23 (right).

Printed in the United States of America at Corporate Graphics in North Mankato, Minnesota.

TABLE OF CONTENTS

PRETTY PETS

Have you ever been to a pet store? **Aquariums** line the walls. Fish of all colors swim in them.

A child picks one out. She takes it home as a pet. All fish used to be wild. Let's find out how they first become pets!

FROM FOOD TO FRIENDS

For more than 8,000 years, people in China have raised fish. But these were not pets. They were food! Farmers likely caught them with nets. The farmers dug **channels** and built ponds for the fish to swim in.

carp

Ancient Romans also raised fish for food. How do we know? Authors wrote about it. **Archaeologists** found **ruins** where fish farms used to be.

fish farm
ruins

People in ancient Egypt and the Middle East may have been the first to keep pet fish. Art shows that they threw hooks with **bait** to catch them.

Ancient Romans were the first to keep **saltwater** fish as pets. They built ponds. They filled them with ocean water. They kept eels and other saltwater fish in them.

DID YOU KNOW?

Some rich Romans kept moray eels as pets. One even decorated his favorite eel with earrings and a necklace!

hooks

moray eel

When they traveled, people brought their pet fish to new places. Goldfish were first kept in China more than 1,000 years ago. They reached Japan in the 1500s. They were in Europe in the 1700s. They made it to the United States by the 1800s.

WHAT DO YOU THINK?

Many fish sold in pet stores today come from Asia. These fish often travel thousands of miles to their new homes. Do you think this is good for the fish? Why or why not?

People began to **breed** pet fish around the globe. In 1869, a French scientist bred a **tropical fish**. It was called the paradise fish. This led to a boom in people owning **exotic** fish. Today, pet stores sell many kinds of tropical fish!

DID YOU KNOW?

People often choose pet fish for their color. It is likely Chinese people first bred fish to have particular colors. This happened more than 1,000 years ago!

paradise fish

CHAPTER 3

FANTASTIC FISH

At first, only rich people owned fish. Why? Fish were expensive. Their aquariums were, too. Over time, more people could afford them. By the 1900s, goldfish were given away as prizes in many countries!

4 BALLS - 4 TICKETS

Goldfish are still popular pets. Why? They are pretty to look at. They come in many colors. They are quiet.

There are more pet fish in the United States today than any other pet. **Freshwater** fish are much more common than saltwater fish. Why? They are easier to care for. They are also less expensive.

TAKE A LOOK!

In which countries do the most people have pet fish?
Take a look!

- ■ China
- ■ United States
- France
- ■ Brazil
- ■ Australia
- United Kingdom
- ■ Germany
- New Zealand
- ■ Italy
- Russia

Aquariums come in many shapes and sizes. People often put plants in them. Why? Fish eat the plants. Plants also give fish places to hide. Rocks and shells do, too.

WHAT DO YOU THINK?

Today's aquariums have **filters** and heat to keep fish healthy. How do you think these are different from the ponds they were first kept in?

Owning pet fish can be good for your health. How? Watching them swim is relaxing. It can help you feel calm. Do you have a pet fish? If not, would you like one?

DID YOU KNOW?

Many scientists say fish have feelings. Fish may also be able to recognize people who feed them.

QUICK FACTS & TOOLS

MOST POPULAR U.S. PET FISH BREEDS

1. guppy

2. molly

3. swordtail

4. betta

5. neon tetra

6. zebra

GLOSSARY

ancient: Belonging to a period long ago.

aquariums: Glass tanks in which fish are kept.

archaeologists: People who study past human lives and activities through remains such as walls, pottery, jewelry, and more.

bait: A small amount of food put on a hook or in a trap to attract fish or other animals.

breed: To keep animals or plants under controlled conditions so they produce more and better quality offspring.

channels: Narrow stretches of water between two areas of land.

exotic: From a faraway country.

filters: Devices in aquariums that clean and aerate the water.

freshwater: Water, such as that found in rivers, ponds, and streams, that does not contain salt.

ruins: The remains of something that has collapsed or been destroyed.

saltwater: Water from the sea or ocean that contains salt.

tropical fish: Any of various small or brightly colored fish that originally came from the tropics.

INDEX

TO LEARN MORE

Finding more information is as easy as 1, 2, 3.

1 Go to www.factsurfer.com

2 Enter "thehistoryofpetfish" into the search box.

3 Choose your book to see a list of websites.

FACT SURFER